How Can I Forgive?

Text copyright © 1990 Vera Sinton
This edition copyright © 1999 Lion Hudson

The author asserts the moral right
to be identified as the author of this work

A Lion Book
an imprint of
Lion Hudson plc
Mayfield House, 256 Banbury Road,
Oxford OX2 7DH, England
www.lionhudson.com
ISBN-13: 978-0-7459-4134-9
ISBN-10: 0-7459-4134-6

First edition 1990
10 9 8 7 6 5 4 3 2 1 0

The text paper used in this book has been made from wood
independently certified as having come from sustainable forests

A catalogue record for this book is available
from the British Library

Typeset in 12/13 Venetian 301
Printed and bound in Malta

How Can I Forgive?

Steps to forgiveness and healing

VERA SINTON

Contents

The unforgivable hurt

Once in a while there is a hurt which stops you in your tracks. You feel shocked, outraged. You may be blazing with anger or just feel cold and numb. The last thing you feel like doing is turning towards the one who hurt you. Perhaps you feel it is impossible to forget the hurt or stop feeling the anger. Perhaps it even seems that it would be wrong to forgive: what has been done offends all justice.

▌A small boy is playing with a stick in an open space just beyond his village. There are still some bones and skulls to be seen in the grass, remains of the last massacre when troops swept in and shot all the people they suspected of helping the guerillas. In the boy's mind, the stick is a machine-gun. He is practising shooting his father's murderers. He is the man of the family now. When he grows up, he has to take revenge.

▌Sixty years on from the second world war, some of the inmates of prisoner-of-war camps in the Asian jungles are still campaigning for compensation. They speak of the lasting physical effects of the torture they went through. 'The world may forget,' one man says, 'but I could never forgive.'

Maybe the unforgivable hurt is to someone you love. Shirley bottled up the hurt done to her husband by a colleague at work. 'I have no problem forgiving for myself,' she said, 'but I feel I have no right to forgive that.'

Forgiveness for the little everyday injuries is something we give and receive all the time.

I tread on your toe and you say, 'That's all right.'

Someone makes a mistake that delays the whole team at work but we smile and carry on.

A comment from a friend suddenly hurts me. She sees my frown or the way my shoulders sag and quickly shows she is sorry and cheers me up. We forgive and are forgiven, hardly noticing it happen.

But what happens when it comes to the big hurts for which there will be no easy cure? How *can* we forgive?

Some people have found an answer to that question.

Forgiving against all odds

In times of war and political unrest, things happen which leave huge scars of unforgiven wrongs. But such times can also produce shining examples of forgiveness.

❙ Pastor Son in Korea in the 1940s was a gentle, gracious man. He had already suffered imprisonment by the foreigners who controlled his country. Then he received news that his two sons at college had been murdered by student activists because they would not join the cause.

As the Pastor took their funeral service, the congregation was astonished to hear him announce that God had given him a love which made him determined to seek out and adopt the killer. Through a network of friends, a frightened young man was rescued from a firing squad and brought face to face with his victims' family. 'We've lost two sons,' said Pastor Son. 'Come and be our son instead.'

❙ In 1987, millions of viewers watched television interviews with Gordon Wilson. He and his daughter were buried in rubble by a bomb blast at a public parade in Northern Ireland. He was holding her hand as she died. But he refused to nurse ill will against the bombers. 'I shall pray for them tonight and every night. God forgive them, for they don't know what they do.'

❚ A Dutch woman, Corrie ten Boom, at the age of fifty was suddenly plunged into the excitement of helping Jews escape the Nazis. As a result, she and her sister Betsie were sent to Ravensbruck concentration camp, where Betsie died. After the war, Corrie worked tirelessly helping people to forgive.

Then came the day when one of those sadistic guards from Ravensbruck stepped up to her with a beaming face. He had found God's forgiveness and wanted to shake her hand. All the horrors of the camp and of her sister's suffering passed before Corrie's eyes. Her arm seemed to be stuck to her side. Silently she prayed, 'Jesus, I cannot forgive him. Give me your forgiveness.'

'As I took his hand,' she writes, 'the most incredible thing happened. From my shoulder along my arm and through my hand a current seemed to pass from me to him, while in my heart sprang a love for this stranger that almost overwhelmed me.'

'Oh, but,' you may be saying, 'those are very special people. I couldn't be like that. I'm not even sure I want to be.'

Of course, you can choose not to forgive. But before you do, it is worth looking at the consequences.

Resentment is bad for you

An English proverb says,

Sticks and stones may break my bones
but words can never harm me.

Alas, that is quite untrue. Words can do untold damage, even at a physical level. When someone deceives you, or curses you, the anger or fear you feel produces profound changes to your heart rate and blood pressure. Your body gears up to fight or run away. In extreme cases, people can suffer heart attacks or strokes as a result of hearing cruel words or watching horrible events.

Pain is an important safety valve. When you cut your leg, the pain you feel warns you of the damage done and reminds you to be more careful. It may send you hurrying to someone you love for consolation. Or to a doctor for stitches.

Feeling anger when you have been hurt by someone is not wrong. (We shall come back to this.) It is a normal reaction and the sign of a healthy personality. If the matter is small and trivial you probably need simply to admit the feeling and quietly bring it under control.

But if it is a more serious hurt you may well need help. The pain should not be ignored. It should be openly admitted to someone else who can comfort and help. It often takes time before emotional pain subsides.

Ideally, talking will be followed by reconciliation with the person who caused the hurt. You say to me, 'You hurt me.' We talk about it until I understand the hurt and show I am sorry about it and want to give you comfort and love.

Usually that will be sufficient to take much of the pain out of the hurt and to start it on the way to speedy recovery, like a wound that has been disinfected, bandaged up and will soon disappear altogether. That is the best kind of healing.

But suppose you refuse to talk or to admit there is a problem. The anger you felt at the beginning does not go away. Instead it settles down into a long-term resentment. Every time you think about the event you smoulder inside. It worms its way into your personality and begins to infect other relationships. 'I'll never trust anyone again,' you say to yourself, and you start to hold more people at arm's length.

If the resentment is strong enough, the inner

stress may take its toll on the body. Every doctor knows patients whose chronic conditions are made worse by unhealed resentment inside. So initial anger may be healthy, but long-term, unhealed anger is very dangerous indeed. For our own good, we need to learn how to forgive.

You are not perfect

We have seen that one reason for forgiving is the inward-looking one: resentment damages yourself. But there is a more outward-looking reason. None of us is perfect. If you are honest you will admit that, like everyone else, you frequently need forgiveness. You need it from other people. You need forgiveness from God.

That last thought may be a new one to you. Your words, your actions are not meaningless. They are not just your private concern. They matter to a God who knows every detail of your inner life.

When you are lazy or untruthful, careless or cutting, greedy or cowardly, you offend the Creator who made you. When you hurt another person, or fail to put your energy and talents to use, you are actually hurting a Father who cares about you and the people around you, like children in his family.

King David in the Bible once arranged the death of one of his best soldiers because he had fallen for the man's wife. When he began to feel guilt about what he had done, he wrote in a poem to God, 'Against you, you only, have I sinned.'

He understood the seriousness of his actions in the eyes of a God who cares.

This may sound gloomy to you, especially if you are feeling sore about how other people have hurt you. But in fact it is only the prelude to good news.

The good news is that God offers you complete forgiveness. And he does it in a way that takes seriously the hurt and damage done by your failure and sin.

God's forgiveness is linked to a real event that took place in history twenty centuries ago but is still immensely relevant today.

Imagine some of the things you would find most difficult to forgive:

I injustice carried out for cynical political ends
I the jealous destruction of a man because of his good influence over others
I being betrayed for money by someone you trusted
I desertion by a close companion at the moment of danger, denying all knowledge of you
I beating someone up for a bit of fun
I allowing an innocent man to be sentenced to one of the cruellest deaths ever devised
I standing and jeering at a person in excruciating pain.

Jesus, God's Son, was the only sinless person who has ever lived. While all these things were happening to Jesus, he was loving the people involved, offering friendship to the one who betrayed him, warning his companions of danger ahead. He gently challenged the governor who sentenced him. He openly prayed for the soldiers who nailed his hands and feet to a cross, 'Father, forgive them, for they do not know what they are doing.'

At the climax of it all he was bearing the full penalty of all the sin committed by people down the centuries. He experienced what it felt like to be out of touch with God, as you and I are. He cried, 'Why have you forsaken me?'

God responded with a unique demonstration of his power over the universe. He raised his Son to life again. Jesus met his followers again and gave them good news to pass on: the offer of forgiveness and new life lived in love with God.

The forgiveness God offers us is not a cheap and easy one.

The philosopher sneered, 'God will forgive. It is his business.'

The cross of Jesus Christ tells another story. God poured out his heart in costly love, sending his beloved Son to die for you and me. He invites you to turn to him and say, 'I am sorry for my sin. I believe Jesus died for me. Please forgive me and make me your son or daughter again.'

But realize, if you take that step, you are also committing yourself to forgive.

The forgiven should forgive

Unforgiving resentment is often compared with the way we feel when someone owes us money. We may fume or nag but that won't help the situation if the debtor has no cash with which to pay.

In most cases where forgiveness is a problem, there is no way that the offender could put things right. It is very rare to be able to make amends exactly. What could ever put right the loss of a son or daughter? Or wipe out the effects of a malicious rumour? The only way forward is for the offended person to accept the loss and agree to cancel the 'debt'.

We have seen that none of us is perfect. We are constantly hurting God. We are hopelessly in his debt and can do nothing but ask for forgiveness. God, however, is overwhelmingly generous. When we ask, he forgives. Through his love on the cross, the debt has been paid.

But there is a condition. It is not a test we pass in order to earn God's love. We can never do that. It is more like a test which reveals whether we have really understood God's love and are truly sorry for our sin.

Jesus put it this way: if we accept God's generous forgiveness of our debt of millions, it is utterly out of keeping to refuse forgiveness to others of a debt of mere hundreds:

Forgive us our debts
as we forgive our debtors.

That comes in the famous prayer that Jesus taught his followers to pray. It was the line he picked out for emphasis afterwards. The God who forgives us requires us to be forgiving people.

We have seen two reasons for forgiving: resentment damages us, and an unforgiving heart grieves God. Now we must look at the steps involved in forgiveness.

Being honest about your anger

'The first step towards forgiveness is to recognize the hurt and be honest with yourself about your feelings.'

The normal human response to hurt is anger, but anger can be expressed in two opposite ways.

▌We can go on the attack: we scold, we criticize, we make threatening gestures. When greatly provoked, we slap or kick or punch.

▌Or we can withdraw. We sulk, we refuse to cooperate. We take things away. We make it clear by our actions that we no longer trust. Silence can be just as aggressive in a quarrel as shouting.

Some people are brought up in families where it is considered wrong for anyone to show signs of anger. They may find it hard to recognize the feeling in themselves.

'I'm not angry,' someone said, clenching her fists and glaring at me. 'You'll never make me angry.'

We often smile as we hear someone shouting, 'I am *not* raising my voice.'

Your anger may be like a raging fire or like an iceberg. In either case, the look on your face, the way you sit or stand, your tone of voice, or the words you choose, will nearly always betray to others that you are angry.

It is important to be able to recognize and identify what you are feeling. Try to describe your feelings as accurately as you can:

I'm disappointed.
I'm feeling irritated.
That makes me furious.
I'm sad and hurt.
My reaction to this mess is to feel shocked and numb.

Recognizing your true feelings is not always as easy as it sounds.

When someone has been very badly hurt by another person, their confidence and inner sense of worth can plummet. The basic anger may be deeply buried under a sense of failure and uselessness. If such a person is rushed into instant forgiving it can be dangerous.

'I'm sorry I stormed out yesterday and spent the holiday money on a computer. You don't really mind, do you?' asked Peter, a little bit too breezily at breakfast. He had come home very late the previous night. There had been no time to talk.

'No, of course not,' replied Helen. 'I know it was my fault for nagging you about the accounts.' But later she was weeping unexpectedly at silly little things. There was a greyness about everything and she felt tired and lacking in energy.

Symptoms like that can be signs that anger is being repressed and the person may be sinking into depression. If Helen cannot tell Peter what she really feels, she needs to talk about it with an experienced friend or counsellor.

'Sorry' is not a magic formula: it must never prevent us from talking about the problems in a relationship and finding real solutions.

If you are a more confident person you may have no difficulty in recognizing the feelings of anger that surge inside when someone hurts you. You may be alarmed by their strength and feel guilty about the feelings.

'Be angry, but do not sin,' the Bible says. The initial feeling is not wrong. Do not waste energy trying to deny it, but use your energy to bring the anger under control and resolve the situation.

One way in which we can always safely express our anger is by taking it to God. Talking to God does not have to be tidied up into neat and respectable prayers. The Bible has many examples of prayers in which people freely air their fears and doubts, their rage at betrayal or injustice.

The small child who rushes in and starts to pummel Daddy in a rage is more likely to find comfort than the one who slinks away and sulks.

God is wonderfully compassionate. Throwing our worst feelings at him can be the first step to finding his help and regaining our peace of mind.

Being realistic about the event

'The second step in the process of forgiveness is to get a clear view of what really happened.'

You may discover that your initial feelings were an overreaction to the situation. It is possible that the mess you are in, the pain or fear you experienced, will begin to look comic.

A sense of humour is a great gift. The most likeable people are those who rarely take offence over a mistake or muddle because they quickly see the funny side of things. Their feelings of anger are converted almost instantly into gales of laughter.

Laughing, of course, will not be right in many situations. But is the alternative always to blame somebody?

A schoolteacher was bitterly upset about failing a driving test. She went over and over it in her mind and was convinced that she had been unjustly assessed.

Behind her anger lay the fact that this woman had never in her life failed an exam. She had an unbroken record of success and this one failure seemed to be a major disaster.

It was easy for onlookers to see she had set herself an unrealistic standard – 'I must never fail' – and that her feelings were a result of that. Learning from experience that it was not a total disgrace to retake a test would be much healthier for her than suing the driving examiner.

'Why do you look at the speck of sawdust in your brother's eye and pay no attention to the plank in your own eye?' asked Jesus with comic exaggeration. He was pointing out a well-known human failing. We tend to notice and criticize in other people the things which are our own most glaring faults.

▋'I cannot stand John,' said Arthur. 'He always tries to dominate the group.'

Poor Arthur was perplexed by the hoots of laughter which erupted round the room. It took some time before we cheered him up. We hope he left a wiser man.

There is a similar problem when feelings creep into the present from previous, unforgiven wrongs.

▋Carol had taken her new boyfriend home to meet her parents.

'Never bring that man to my house again,'

her father ordered. 'He has crossed a strikers' picket line.'

It was years since Carol's father had spoken of his anger and disappointment about the long and damaging strike that had cost him his job. Carol thought he had forgiven the managers. Now she discovered that all his bitterness was focused on workers who betrayed their cause.

We have seen that when something makes us angry, the strength of those feelings may come from our past history, or from unrealistic expectations. We need to learn to understand ourselves in order to avoid putting unfair blame on others.

Seeing the other person's view

❝Now that you have a clear understanding of what has happened and how you feel about it, the next stage is to try to understand the other person's point of view.❞

The French have a saying,

> To understand everything
> is to forgive everything.

There is much truth in that: when you understand, the problem may evaporate. But it is not the whole story. Understanding is the step that shows us which things can be excused and which things need to be forgiven.

Once I understand what it was like for you when you hurt me, I may say:

I can see it was an accident.
It was just a misunderstanding – a muddle.
It was nobody's fault.
You were under such pressure you couldn't help it.
You couldn't have known I would be offended.

Having understood everything, I excuse you.

It is as if my inner court of justice has pronounced, 'There is no case to be tried.'

On the other hand, having understood everything, I may blame you:

You were careless.
You did not try to understand.
You were inefficient.
Despite the stress, you could have had more self-control.

When we blame someone's action we are saying to them, 'You are a mature person. You know there are things that are right and wrong in the world. You are able to make choices. I hold you responsible for this action.'

If we excuse something that was blatantly wrong we are saying to the offender, 'I have low expectations of you. I despise you. I do not consider you worth my moral indignation.'

Once we have excused all that needs to be excused, once we have discovered what it is that needs to be blamed, then we may be ready to say:

Yes, you did this thing. I accept your apology. I will not hold this against you. I will trust you as I did before.

At this point, we face the full cost of forgiving. It may well be beyond us.

The role of love

Let's look at the steps so far.

❚ Someone has hurt you.

❚ You know what has happened and how you feel about it.

❚ You understand how the other person felt and you can partly excuse them.

❚ But there is still something wrong and you blame them for that.

Now, how do you find the power and the will to forgive?

Do you fear that it cannot be done, that things will never be the same again?

Do you make it depend on the other person? If they apologize nicely and make you feel really generous you will forgive.

Does it depend on how much you care about them or need them?

Love provides a very strong motive for forgiving.

If we know we love someone we do not easily let them go. If they are dear to us and we care for them, we cannot throw them away like worn-out clothes. To lose them is more like cutting off a finger. We may be very angry with them and feel that forgiving is going to be hard and hurt us. But we also know that in the long run it will hurt us more to lose their love.

Most of us learn how to forgive when we are children. We learn it with parents and guardians whom we love and deeply need. We are very busy learning new things. All the time we fail and make mistakes. It is the experience of being loved and forgiven which helps us to grow and become loveable people.

We soon learn that the adults are not perfect either. They sometimes admit that they are wrong, and we forgive. This brings us even closer together: we feel safe.

But maybe for some reason you learned that lesson badly in childhood. You do not feel as if love can safely overcome hurt. And now you find it hard to trust and hard to forgive. If that is the case you may need to talk it over with someone. It is never too late to learn better ways to love.

But warm feelings of love are not the full story. We cannot have a close relationship with everyone. Yet God tells us to love them. Jesus sums up all that God requires in these two commands:

Love the Lord your God with all your heart, soul, mind and strength. Love your neighbour as yourself.

Here loving means recognizing every person as precious and valuable to God – as precious as we are. It is a basic attitude from which the feelings of love may develop as we get to know a person.

❙ When Gordon Wilson first declared that he forgave the bombers who killed his daughter, he did not know who they were or how much they were to blame. He was just beginning to feel the terrible pain of losing the daughter he loved. Many steps in the process of forgiveness lay ahead.

What he was doing was declaring his belief that those bombers are precious human beings loved by God, however guilty they may be. He was expressing his belief that it would be possible to forgive.

❙ When Pastor Son declared he wanted to adopt his sons' killer, he trusted God to bring a new beginning out of pain and death. He trusted a God whose love can make us loving and loveable.

Deep in our hearts, most of us share that belief that all human beings are of value, even though they fail. When something terrible happens and we feel the desire for hate and revenge, all our faith and values are challenged. We may draw back and ask, is it right in *this case* to forgive?

When forgiveness seems unjust

'Surely there are times when it is wrong to forgive? You may feel it is one thing to forgive injury to yourself but quite different when the event caused hurt to others. What would happen to justice if we all forgave?'

In 1986 three men broke into a home in West London, searching for money. Finding little of value they grew angry. Two of them brutally raped the daughter of the house. Her boyfriend and her father were tied up and beaten with a sports bat.

The immediate reaction of this Christian family was to forgive. 'At the time it happened, forgiveness was natural,' said the girl in a radio interview. 'Later I had to work it out. I knew that not forgiving would destroy me.'

Eleven months later the three men were in court. The judge gave much lighter sentences for the rape than for the robbery. The family had overcome their ordeal well, he said. So he decided the victim's suffering had not been so bad.

The father protested most strongly that this

was unjust. For him there was no contradiction between saying personally, 'I forgive them,' and also demanding that the justice of the law be fully carried out.

Parents often withhold forgiveness from a child for a period of time while the child is scolded or punished. Once that is over, in a good family everything returns to normal. The fault is forgotten and the child is encouraged and loved.

In the adult world the state needs to have rules and penalties. It is important that justice is done.

Punishment should be measured out fairly. A person in authority may feel great love and sympathy for an offender and long to give them a free pardon. But he or she has to weigh up very carefully how that would affect other people.

If we look at a bully and say, 'Poor thing. He couldn't help it. He had a bad childhood,' we send a message to his victims that they are not being valued and protected. We may also be undervaluing the offender, implying we despise him and have low expectations.

The New Testament records how the apostle Paul was once thrown into prison in Philippi, after the magistrates had had him beaten up.

Next morning they sent a message that he was to be released. But Paul knew his rights under Roman law.

He could have forgiven the magistrates and left quietly. He had often written letters to people urging them to be generously forgiving. In this case, however, he sat firmly in prison until the magistrates came to apologize.

Forgiveness is at the heart of the Christian faith, but so too is justice.

Forgiveness must never be used as an easy way out of a situation of conflict. We all have a duty to be brave in upholding justice in the world.

Saying 'I'm sorry'

❛She said: 'Of course I'll forgive him, but he ought to come and see me. Why should I make the first move?'

He said: 'I long to apologize, but I don't dare to call on her. She'll tear me apart.❜

So far we have mainly looked at forgiveness from the viewpoint of the person who has been hurt.

If a relationship is to be fully restored, forgiveness is only one half of the process. It is necessary for the one who has done the injury to be sorry.

Forgiveness matched with repentance produces reconciliation.

Forgiveness is:
❚ granting free pardon for a hurt
❚ giving up all claim for compensation
❚ ceasing to feel resentment

Repentance is:
❚ accepting a pardon for a hurt
❚ making any appropriate restitution

❚ ceasing to feel guilt and shame

Repentance can be quite as hard as forgiveness. It follows similar steps:

❚ Repentance involves coming to terms with feelings. Guilt and shame burn as strongly as feelings of hurt and anger. Some people tend to bury them and refuse to admit any fault. Some overreact and punish themselves with destructive remorse.

❚ *Repentance means understanding why the other felt hurt.* An event will never look quite the same to the different people involved in it.

❚ *Repentance requires respect and love for the other.* 'Hasn't he a sense of humour?' 'Why is she making such a fuss?' For the offender to treat a hurt as trivial or a joke undervalues the one offended.

A problem that often arises with reconciliation is the question, is a public apology appropriate?

Should confession be public?
'Dorothy, my dear, I feel I really must apologize to you. I have been thinking such horrible things about you since I saw you eating with Clifford

the other day. I am sure it was quite innocent. Please forgive my jealous mind.'

There is a nasty danger that an apology can be a subtle way of conveying to someone else the anger or criticism we feel about them.

Someone has suggested as a good principle that confession should be as public as the act committed.

Private hurtful thoughts that have not already been given away by looks and gestures should remain our own business.

A clearly wrong action – for example, a theft that has put other people under suspicion – needs public confession to clear away the blame.

An act of adultery can be a difficult case, something intensely private but involving one or two other people.

Don had always been faithful to Elsa and she trusted him. He deeply regretted his night in Vienna when loneliness drove him to look for a woman. He longed to tell Elsa and get her forgiveness and comfort.

But he suspected she would be devastated and find it hard to trust him on trips again. And she would start worrying about disease. These days you can never tell when that might catch up with you. He was worried, himself, about the thought of an HIV test. If he did not tell Elsa, then he must carry the burden himself. It seemed extremely unlikely she would find out, but, if she did, things would be even worse.

Decisions about confession have to balance the relief and healing it can bring to us against the shock and pain it may cause to others.

Failure and wrong can always be confessed to God. The best starting point for repentance is prayer. Putting aside damaged pride, we can come into the presence of the Lord,

> *who is compassionate and gracious,*
> *slow to anger and abounding in love;*
> *who does not treat us as our sins deserve*
> *or repay us according to our fault.*

Once you are reconciled with him, rely on his help to find the wisest way to be reconciled with others.

When there is no response

‘What if the guilty party does not say 'I'm sorry'? Can forgiving work if it is one-sided?’

Forgiving the defiant

Without response from the other side we cannot restore a relationship. We may find we cannot be at peace with someone, but even in war we can love. God does.

> Love your enemies and pray for your persecutors;
> only so can you be children of your heavenly Father,
> who causes the sun to rise on good and bad alike.

We can go through the early steps of forgiveness:
I feeling our hurt and anger
I understanding what happened
I valuing the other person.

Then we can make a commitment to love which means refusing to let ourselves nurse thoughts of hatred and revenge. If we meet an enemy who is hungry, we feed him. If we meet one who is wounded, we bandage her up. But if we meet him attacking and causing damage, we use all the energy our anger gives us to prevent and restrain him.

Love can be gentle and compassionate, but love can also be energetic with moral indignation. Jesus showed these two sides of love very well.

He was so welcoming to the hurt people in society, the failures that other people despised.

He was openly indignant with the self-righteous people who laid heavy burdens on the poor, hardly noticing what they were doing.

Anger serves a good purpose when it rescues others or sets us back on our feet.

As soon as it becomes triumphant, lifting us above the other person, it is dangerous.

As soon as it becomes redundant, unable to change anything for the good, we need to let it go.

Forgiving the dead

The family members were furious with the undertaker. Why had he booked George's funeral so early in the morning?

What they were really angry about was having to come out and look sad about George's death, when they had all been wishing him dead for years.

Anger and guilt get muddled up together with shock and grief when someone who has hurt you dies. In this situation, anger serves no helpful purpose. Make a decision, and let it go.

But take time over the process. There is no hurry now. Feel your grief and feel your rage. Release the burden into God's hands. Work gradually back to restore the memory of a person who was at times respected and loved. Be thankful for things that were good and for things you learned, even in pain.

Forgiving in a divorce

An abandoned wife or husband will need time to feel the indignation at the way their partner has treated them, in order to keep a true view of what happened and avoid self-despair.

But for the children it is different. They need to be reconciled with their missing father or mother, and to be allowed to go on loving them.

Divorce may be even harder than a bereavement. The same process must take place: grieving, raging, letting go.

But all the time there is the danger that new contact over family matters or money will bring the conflict back to life again.

Neither innocent nor guilty

'Don't tell me there are no innocent parties in a marriage break-up,' Anna said.'

I understood her indignation. She was at the height of bewilderment and grief over the nastiness of her husband's departure after twenty-five years of marriage.

But, at the end of the day, I *do* want to tell Anna that there is no such thing as an innocent and a guilty party if a couple want to achieve a reconciliation.

When two people have shared themselves deeply in love they expose themselves in all their faults and weaknesses. They are vulnerable to endless hurt, as well as open to great joy.

Forgiveness is not just sorting out the past and laying it to rest. Forgiveness is reaffirming trust. It is saying:

I will continue to be open with you.
I will not erect barriers to protect myself.
You have the freedom to fail again and still be forgiven.

We cannot mould those we love to fit our needs exactly. There will be many hurts in love.

It is not only in marriage that it is hard to draw a clear line between offender and offended. In many other relationships we hurt others as quickly as we are hurt ourselves.

'How many times do I have to forgive someone?' the apostle Peter once asked Jesus. 'Seven times seven?' 'No, no,' said Jesus. 'Seventy times seven. Try counting that.'

A word of warning here: forgiveness does not always mean returning to where you were. Sometimes hurts occur because you have been allowing a friend to make too many demands on you. Part of the process of reconciliation should be to admit this and start to say no to those demands.

That is also a risky process. Your friend may find it hard to accept new limits. You may be accused of being unforgiving. It may take much hard work before your relationship with that person begins to flourish again. Perhaps it never will. Love includes the goodwill, if need be, to let someone go.

Friend again, or permanent debtor?

Real forgiveness means giving up all claim to compensation. But genuine repentance involves some real attempt to put matters right.

If you believe that people matter more than things, making payments or doing tasks can never be seen as making up for a hurt. There is a generosity at the heart of forgiveness. The pardon should be free. There should be no continuing claim.

Jack said he forgave his brother for the reckless driving that cost him the use of his legs. But as the months spent pushing a wheelchair rolled on into years, Dick began to feel he was being asked to pay and pay.

Oh, to be very rich! Then he could pay Jack compensation and leave home for ever, free of this endless burden.

Was Jack imposing the burden, or did Dick take it on himself?

If the forgiving person should be generous, it is right that, within reason, the repenting person should make amends.

Forgiveness is phoney if it leaves either person

feeling morally superior.

If the forgiver refuses all reasonable offers of help and dominates the other person, making them feel forced to be grateful, that is false forgiveness.

If the forgiven person dominates by insisting on making enormous payments or sacrificial efforts to earn forgiveness, that is false repentance.

If these dangers are to be avoided, it is important not to rush the process of forgiveness. Start it quickly, but take time to make sure that both sides know what is being offered and where responsibility ends.

The power to forgive

We have looked at the steps to forgiveness:
I recognizing the hurt and anger
I understanding what has happened and how the other person views it
I letting the anger go.

Perhaps you have taken each of these steps yourself.

But simply knowing the steps and understanding the problem will not make the hurt go away. Sooner or later you must make the decision to forgive and commit yourself to the costly way of love.

How can it be done? How can you summon up the power to do something as difficult as this?

We have already said that God expects those he forgives to be forgiving. He *commands* us to forgive. But he does not expect us to do it on our own. If we genuinely want to forgive the wrong done to us, he promises us his help.

As Corrie ten Boom and millions like her have discovered, when you reach out to forgive, trusting God, he gives that power. You have only to ask:

I cannot forgive this person. Please enable me to forgive.

As you pray that prayer and make that decision, act on it. Determine not to nurse your hurt. Don't wait for the other person; make the first move. When you talk to other people, speak lovingly of the person you have forgiven. If resentment creeps back into your thoughts, remind yourself that you have wiped the record clean — as God has done for you. The wound has been cleaned and stitched. It is healing. You are free.